AF334546

# Those I Guard

# Those I Guard

POEMS BY

*Karl*

*Kirchwey*

HARCOURT BRACE & COMPANY

San Diego   New York   London

Library of Congress Cataloging-in-Publication Data
Kirchwey, Karl, 1956–
Those I guard: poems/by Karl Kirchwey. —1st ed.
p.  cm.
ISBN: 0-15-190170-8
ISBN: 0-15-690120-X (pbk.)
I. Title.
PS3561.I684T48   1993
811'.54—dc20          93-12729

Designed by Trina Stahl
Printed in the United States of America
First edition
A B C D E

To the memory of my father,
George W. Kirchwey III
1920–1988

# Contents

# *Acknowledgments*

Poems in this book have appeared (sometimes in different form) in the following periodicals, to whom grateful acknowledgment is made:

*Antaeus*: "The Transformation of Light"

*Boulevard*: "The Crocus"

*Harvard Magazine*: "Interior, Sunday Afternoon"

*The Kenyon Review*: "For the Assassins," "Stanzas from the Life of George Fox, 1651–1662"

*The Literary Review*: "Between Roscoe and Absarokee"

*The Nation*: "Murray Hill Barbershop," "Rhône Valley, after Rain," "The Spider's Art"

*The New Criterion*: "Natural History"

*The New Republic*: "Saint Rock"

*The New Yorker*: "Crystal Ice Company," "Saint Nicholas," "Rogue Hydrant, August," "Lest He Put Forth His Hand"

*The Paris Review*: "Liberators," "An Aside at the Met," "Trout Tank, Café Le Sporting," "Aubade, Deer Isle"

*Prairie Schooner*: "Buoy 32A," "Moonrise, Indian Wells Beach, Amagansett"

*The Southwest Review*: "Decline and Fall"

*Western Humanities Review*: "Two Studies of Lesbos (after Thucydides)," "The Snow Sphinx"

*The Yale Review*: "Memnon"

I know that I shall meet my fate
Somewhere among the clouds above;
Those that I fight I do not hate,
Those that I guard I do not love . . .

> —W. B. YEATS,
> "An Irish Airman Foresees His Death"


Say that they mattered, alive and after;
That they gave us time to become what we could.

> —RICHARD WILBUR

# I

---

# Crystal Ice Company

These grow beneath rusty plates, with brine
circulating and ammonia saturnine
in the nostrils. Slowly the brooding poisons calve
into substantial clarities. He moves
among submerged lights which are weak,
as a low smoke or planetary cowlick
might fume across a lost explorer's lenses;
then in the acrid damp he stops, remembers

*Port Washington, a winter dawn, 1928:*
*as he climbs Beacon Hill in the milkman's cart,*
*a plug of cream sucked from the broken foil top*
*of a bottle lights his face like a buttercup.*

In the end, no airy pinions may remain,
no galactic rose at the center to lessen
the density with imperfections of surface,
no stalled titanium plume; and a steady pulse
of bubbles will ensure this, ticking through.

*The last summer before the divorce, sixty years ago.*
*They are loading rocksalt into the outer sleeve.*
*The crank turns, an unhurried passage of*
*Sunday evening into confections of cream and fruit.*

It is time to vacuum the last impurities out
of the closing heart. Soon rusty chains will raise
three hundred pounds of perfectly made ice
in a groaning transit, a crystal martyrdom
across the cutting floor, ice waiting for him
at the loading dock, bearded with excelsior,
shining, diminished by the hand of summer air.

# Hudson, P. Q., Canada

(A PHOTOGRAPH)

In this case it is July, 1959.
Three years old, I stand by the shackled wedge
of the ferry. But I am not alone:
hand on my shoulder, weight and privilege,

this summer morning my father stands with me.
Before long, we will both set off across
the Lake of Two Mountains—actually
the Ottawa River, widening where it nears

union with the St. Lawrence at Montréal.
I do not understand the meaning of
our crossing this lake (not a lake at all),
leaving behind the smug Scots-English enclave

where we are islanded all round by French-
speaking strangers. My father's eldest son,
I only know we are bound on a voyage,
and do not feel the Heraclitean

flow of the world on whose familiar shores
we live. We have a small errand: to buy,
it might be, a pale disc of Oka cheese
from Trappists over at their priory,

or to negotiate for puppy love
(a wayward black Labrador we will call
Loki) with silent Indians who live
also on that far shore. Though we both smile,

black spirits will guide me across a dead
lake, out of childhood to an anchorage
radically unfixed, still not understood;
nor will I gain clairvoyance with my age,

become adept at seeing past that hazy
shore into a future which will bring loss.
The battered tire-plates have been worn shiny
with passage, and gleam dully through lacunas

and rainbow patternings of motor oil.
The sullen lake, the gapped chains, do not move.
I ought to wear that grimace with which Brunel
poses against the brutal iron weave

of man-sized shackles for his *Great Eastern*
at anchor, behemoth stayed by the language
of power. World-mastering Victorian,
how did I dare set off without such knowledge?

*November 22, 1963*

I was sitting in an empty classroom,
having already been held back one grade,
and I was writing, the anxiety
of language upon me, experience
now and then breaking through the linked dance of
symbols, as if somebody had just come
into the room with a news bulletin
from the radio, events far away.

    In the south the way was clear,
    past the Adolphus Hotel,
    Thomsen Furniture Mart, the
    First National Bank, Walgreen
    Drugs, the windows and signs of
    an idea: twelve dollars
    and seventy-eight cents for
    a Mannlicher-Carcano.

Above the blackboard, proper examples
of cursive script flew away on birds' wings,
and my hand learned to trap something inside,
though I did not understand what, just as
I ran out under the long school porch that
Friday afternoon, sent home early, a
sense of jubilee in my heart because
something extraordinary had happened.

    Her pink suit with its black trim
    was like a burned rose, or the
    exclamation of brain mist
    on the pavement as he grew
    heavier and heavier

6

in her arms, and time seemed to
stand still. Through the live oak leaves,
pigeons rose, wheeled and scattered.

Somehow I have come to live in the world
by means of certain days and events I
no longer recall, except sometimes in
fugitive traces of exultation
or shame. Certain kinds of knowledge are
intolerable, I know this now, though
history contrives, by tutelary
shapes, looped, moving ahead, to draw us on.

Scott-Foresman Rolling Readers,
ten to a box, and the smell
of dust prickling his nostrils
like the first day of school. He
curled himself around absence
and closed his fingers gently
in the late November light
till it begot more absence.

# *Liberators*

One year we lived in the suburbs
in a house built in the 1950's,
that era of civil defense.
It had a bomb shelter in the basement
with a quality of darkness within darkness,
and an arched ceiling of corrugated steel,
like the Nissen huts he lived in
at Wendling during the war.

There were nights he woke up screaming.
Once again the crooked black threads
would flee across the indifferent
bowl of the sky (imperfections
of adult vision) as he hung
in the sling of the turret. Then a single
thread would unravel in an instant,
an impact, a flash, a shriek

of Duralumin, into knowledge greater
than anything he knew or wanted to know.
Crawling forward along a catwalk,
the bomb bay underneath him
flooded with high-octane fuel,
he arrived in the cockpit just in time
to see the copilot beheaded
by a twenty-millimeter cannon shell.

We often went down there to play,
and rubbed the heels of our hands
into our eyes until the light
exploded behind our eyelids
in crawling retinal patterns.

And sometimes darkness, like an ancient
sea, would cast up a fleece-lined
aviator's mitten, a web belt, khaki overalls.

We lay in the darkness till panic
took shape in us, like the pure cold
of thirty thousand feet, or coagulant
dread, taught to flow in a channel
of dreams; like the fountain of learning
he could not stop. Then we groped, clutching
these souvenirs, toward where baffles
hid the daylight, by which we were blinded.

# Grim Reapers

(IN MEMORY OF K.W. K., JR., 1921–1944)

I bought a patch for Fighting Squadron Ten,
  and thought to sew it on the bomber jacket
  over my heart,
where the pocket New Testament had been,

a volume bound in just the Navy blue
  his Hellcat fighter plane was painted with,
  paper and cloth
riding the juggernaut of bombs, alu-

minum and gasoline off the wood deck
  into a future of uncertainty,
  stupendously
alive with hazard. He never came back;

having struggled into the middle air,
  the Word faltered and plunged into the waste
  salt ocean, lost
on his lips in a burst of ack-ack fire

off Saipan, a smudged plume of burning grease.
  His wing man followed him all the way down,
  saw him go in
and not climb out (no chute, no marker dyes),

and was himself killed in the long parade
  of hostile names: Jaluit, Truk and Yap,
  so death tucked up
the one remaining loose narrative thread,

and there is no one left alive to tell
          what happened that June day, to point out where,
          beneath the clear
water, his cockpit gunsight has been all

jeweled with small sponges and colored algae;
          where he still leans into his straps, as if
          in a last dive,
but dreaming now of possibility,

like the girl's face sketched on a plotting chart,
          blooming as the points of the compass rose
          explode across
the emptiness of discipline and habit.

What fascinated him was killing power
          tempered by reflexes and light control.
          Flight made him feel
balanced between self-certainty and fear,

and therefore most himself. My name is his,
          and I will come to the same knowledge he
          did, differently,
though, learning by slower chronologies.

Surely we know the same things in the end.
          That semiliterate itemized list
          a shipboard typist
prepared so many years ago to send

back to his next-of-kin with his few things
          (lighter, wristwatch, bars of a new lieutenant,
          watercolor paints,
a now-unplayable souvenir voice recording,

officer's club card for a captured atoll)
          cannot describe him, any more than this
          insignia's
skeleton diving with a scythe at full

port arms, grinning, in aviator goggles, on
          a circular field of bloodthirsty red.
          Uncle is dead.
I will not wear the patch. It is not mine.

# Trout Tank, Café Le Sporting

They are there in every weather
in my imagination,
as they were in the mountain town
where I was a student once,
in a café declared out-of-bounds
because of sex, drinking and dance.

They are nosing the cloudy walls
of the tank with their gaping mouths and flat
unspeculative eyes. Green and rose
smokes of blood and jealousies limber out
into rainbows, bent from their flanks' follicles
like eruptions of dumb adolescence,

rust or verdigris blooming on gunmetal's
unpolished curve. Sometimes, plastered
with leaves after autumn storms, the tank chills
the air into beads of pure longing
that run down in hesitant trails
and lose themselves at the bottom;

sometimes the snow is heaped up
in a shrug on the tank in December
like a hunched coat, set to ignore
small crises of feeling, abrupt
departures and all the rituals
that will hardly outlast the New Year;

sometimes, with its hidden source
of light, this world seems to tiger
the temperate faces of those
who are waiting on the other side
of the glass, where the horsechestnut's candles
of flower and the twirling panels

depicting ice cream confections
in full color disguise the blind inquiry
that has lasted since childhood and longer,
something that will outlast me,
something glimpsed through a bridal veil
of bubbles: a trophy, a dark gun,

a flush on the throat, a gleam of ruby
in the serpentine of the Gotthard
being worn down to the valley,
excruciating and slow,
ornamented by constant desire.
Something drifts; something waits pitilessly.

# My Father Considered
## as the God of Light

Today we are on Mount Kynthos
in the clothes-dryer heat of August.
It is twenty minutes to eleven in the morning,
according to the watch on my wrist.
We must have woken early to come here,
because overnight stays are prohibited
on the sacred island of Delos.
No one is born here, and no one dies here.

My father is six months a widower.
He is wearing a madras shirt
"bought before Hitler's War."
Beneath the sheen of the cotton,
panels of rust are shot through
with lines of sunlight and azure,
like the sides of the tanker that swings
at her chain down in the empty harbor.

The boat that brought us is elsewhere.
Surely it will come back soon.
Behind us, the tongues of land
alternate with thirsty ultramarine
all the way to the horizon,
which is vague and endless with concealing
what it has always concealed
from those who try to return.

Apollo was born on this island.
His mother lay bearded with papyrus,
screaming in the muddy shallows
as he was coaxed from the darkness
where her maidenhead had closed around the bright stem.
In a moment perfectly balanced
against the incursions of history,
a god was brought into time.

For thirty centuries it has been the same here,
the sunlight battening on massive walls
as tents of blue shadow diminish around us.
My father looks amazed by the heat.
There is a splayed hand of earth on my shoulder,
like an atlas page lying open
to the archipelago of true feeling;
but my father has clothed himself in distance.

# *Buoy 32A*

A depth of seventy-nine feet, the tide running
out, the sun just off the meridian, a mild
day in spring. The boat slows. We have already cast
astern our sprigs of rosemary; it is still too
early for drinks before lunch.

        She opens what looks
like an ordinary paint can; I start to read
from *The Book of Common Prayer*, but the gravel
glimmers and is quickly past, outstripping my words,
a plume of gray in the drab waters of mid-Sound,
unreflective except for occasional darts
of light which do not begin to reach bottom. Swirls
of pollen marble the olive face of it like
endpapers of a book, enclosing winter leaves
miles from shore.

        It is Saint Paul who assures us that
what is sown is not the body of what will be:
rains this spring, for example, having been heavy,
mean that October's apples will be few and small.

The wind drops; conversation drops; and a rime of
pollen gathers at our nostrils, at the corners
of our eyes, so heavy in the air that nature
seems to darken and sleep at the horizon for
a moment, considering what we have added
before passing on.

He may live over the whole
face of the water, in the glistening clumps of
landward weed, in the rapt fiddlehead of gold dust,
and it may be only a failure of vision
that we are unable to so tincture our lives
with this simple paste of seawater and ash that
it once more assumes a kind of galvanic life,

such as what we know waits for the sullen plume to
fall, the dark furrow that waits for the dust to fall
in random patterns. We turn to a catered lunch.

*May 18, 1989*

# II

# Natural History

The jewelers' windows have been muted with
black felt, their crystal riot locked away
for one more night. And yet, so profligate,
so close-set is their unrelenting blaze,
that, after dark, imagination brings
its own combustion, worn to one blood-red
cabochon by the friction of its passage.

*How many hands are worn away with toil*
*so that a single knuckle shines resplendent?*
Silica dust sharpens and clouds the air
from somewhere high above, like snow wind-driven
across a pristine landscape of spruce tips.
But in the risky sandstone vineyards and
arbors of pomegranate finials

five stories up, there are two midway angels
whose only thoughts are barnacled with earth.
They bring a local weather with them (rain),
although the blinking sign above them reads
AUGUST FIFTH 10:00 PM TOMORROW: FAIR.
Their oilskins whicker as they shift along
the narrow scaffold, and their arc lamps veer

madly. Their backs are to the world of sense.
They mix the common sand with water struck
from the brass bole of a standpipe. Their hands
are turned against the vegetable stone,
which holds no ransom for them anymore.
They are trying to drive their shadows from the wall.
By dawn, with filthy tears, they will succeed.

# Rogue Hydrant, August

Morning. The sun gleams wickedly on chrome:
neuralgic intimations for the day.
Up from those stone vaults where the boiler men
in beaked quartz masks wield their erratic torches
on mudlegs, coils and firebrick, erupts
this vengeful glossolalia, to scour
a rank pot liquor from the granite curb
(turds, chewing gum, butts, sputum, wilted flowers),
led from upstate through locomotive-sized
conduits, with the thumb of gravity
pressing and pressing on a glassy core.

A wino from the traffic island puts
insouciant lips down to the furious stream
(two hundred p.s.i. through ductile iron),
his thirst, for once, not dropsical enough
to quench the music of this braided storm.
Oh to lie down, he thinks, and feed upon
this foggy clout and, as at some old loom,
study the gauzy cadence of release,
weaving itself forever fresh and new,
cross-rhythmed, flashing high and low (just like
that nearby boxtop game of three-card monte):

I *will* lead me beside stiller waters than these,
where chance is pastured greenly—and swoons closer.
Too close! It rolls him off, with crystal knives
break-dancing all around. But, for one instant,
he's balanced on the cusp of pleasure's tooth,
buried a hundred years beneath the pavement;
then grovels back through oscillating rings

of perfect clarity, through chlorinated
precincts of freshness, to the muggy street.
He wakes, stands, and vaguely wanders away
just as the water-blue squad car arrives.

# Murray Hill Barbershop

Kostas is back. He's been in hospital
following unexpected surgery.
Six pints, he says he needed, but transfuses
a fatalist's good cheer as usual.
Snapshot: old man by cyclopean wall,
bent, dressed in black. Kostas murmurs that this is
his father, who lived to 103.

Talk is of Greece. Kostas left forty years
ago, and came via Sesto San Giovanni.
But rents, he says, are too high; someday he'll
close up for good. Already the furrier's
moved out, leaving just the supercilious
cookbook store owner, juggling fusilli
and roadmaps in some Byzantine display.

Here nothing changes: the bygone hairstyles
in tacked-up photos; the blue jar (marked "Jervis
Disinfecting Systems") just matching the bay
of Sifnos in that postcard; the tonsorial
modishness of tonics—Lilac Vegetal,
Aqua Velva, VO5, Zetar, Vitalis—
to be recalled, not by aroma, but by

radio jingles last heard in 1960.
Unshaven himself, Kostas plucks a razor
from where it has been marinating, idle
in that great jar, and starts to sing the praises
of Kalamata olives, or retsina's
uncultured tang. Gold lights up in his smile
like the group shot by the Hagia Sofia:

a long-ago vacation, history
ambiguous in its pleasures. He walks soundless
across the pelt of some wild animal,
pauses, and by degrees grows voluble
with how the Greek runner Pheidippides
from Marathon breasted that last long hill.
One word breaks from him now, and it is "victory."

*Two Studies of Lesbos*

(AFTER THUCYDIDES)

———

*for Henri Cole*

1. Aeolian Capitals

(CLEON SPEAKS)

A scholar remarks that they "seem to take no harm,
alive in the sunlight near a *pavillon de danse,*
being carved from a hard, light granite." It is tempting
to let mere words move you, like that yarn of Callimachus
at the tomb of a free-born maiden of Corinth:
how he saw the acanthus creep around the funeral basket
and its covering tile (little things that gave the girl pleasure
when she was alive, left there by her devoted nurse)
and it occurred to him to carve them into a capital,
earning him renown for delicacy and refinement.

A pretty story. But consider instead the adamant
of these obsolete Aeolian capitals,
these sullen nestlings of Zeus in dull Mytilene.
It is summary action promised by that mad mica gaze
("The pad of the abacus droops across beetle brows"),
originally fixed in some peasant's wall
to observe the coupling of horses, and now flipping skirts,
the rhythm of heels—doomed for pleasure, maybe,
but not for posterity: a gaze that withers speech,
that falls on your body like a fist or a granite smile,
engorged with sap, goggle-eyed, resisting time,
like an unforgiving ancient king's, deaf to the claims
of pity or decency or a clever argument.

26

2. City Planning

(DIODOTUS SPEAKS)

Vitruvius is unequivocal:
the city is poorly situated,
lying promiscuously open to the winds,
to Auster, from fever's south,
bringing tigerish quartans;
to Corus, bringing coughs,
and Septentrio, heavy cold
from due north, so that the chief end
of city life is thwarted:
men cannot talk in the streets.

The winds are unanimous.
They walk the country end to end
and carry the sound of goat bells
from Molyvos to the mares grazing
at peace in their seaward pastures
near the broken cistern of radium baths
abandoned at Skala Efthalou;
from the breathless hinterland
to the citrus groves at Eressos
where midges stung Sappho awake;

from the deep wisteria arbors
to where oleander in its dress of white
and crimson chokes the ruined keep
of the Gattelusi fortress,
and the ancient theater is silent in its grove
(pine needles hush each footfall),
except for the voices of cicadas

27

that rise and fall like the voices
of the elders above the Scaean Gates,
and the signs warn of vipers, φίδια.

Tell me, what is the source of the winds?
They arise as incurably
as passions do in men,
and though they depart with a whisper,
there is nothing that can resist them,
not even the cold cast shadow of faith.
Tell me, where shall we build the citadel,
whatever its good taste and magnificence,
that does not turn one open face
toward the whole compass rose of infirmity?

## An Aside at the Met

(ATTIC KRATER, ATTRIBUTED TO LYDOS)

Hera, you may recall, once bore a son
so puny that she dropped him in disgust
off high Olympus, much as, I read just
last week, a teen mother dropped her child down

the incinerator chute to risk the blades
and fire that lay below. (His lusty cries
awoke the decent dozing operators
of the machine in time; he was adopted

by the old lady living in 2A.
But I digress.) The blunt immortal babe
survived, grew, and in school did best at shop
(A$^+$ for metalworking) to repay

her cruelty by fashioning a chair
whose arms would close around her and then lock,
making her briefly the gods' laughingstock
as she struggled. Though he fell like a star,

morning till evening, out of heaven to
bare Lemnos (this time Zeus gave him the heave),
Hephaestus limped back in a bacchic weave—
in just *this* lurching and wine-soaked review

or cotillion, done some five centuries
before Christ's birth, in black figure. You might
say pleasure learns to be immortal in it.
Now it is I who sink as gravity's

29

gold arms close round me, Dionysos potent
with wine and flutes, and sit. In '31,
as Docent here, I once taught Lewisohn
Dance School students. I have seen no more triumphant

response to beauty, not before or since;
the class simply transformed, a chain of satyrs
and maenads wound through my mundane lecture,
their hands and feet raised, angled in the dance,

pressing at their humanity as though
it were an infant's caul, and with their fawn
glances, their bodies like tendrils of vine,
they dressed the mighty cheeks of that clay bellows,

not lame humans, that moment, but gods, lambent.
The ancient Curator was passing by,
as luck would have it, and saw their revelry
and cried, "Lydos! Lydos!" and "Excellent,

but badly lit!" then limped across the gloom
in search of a custodian to send
into the gray empyrean of paned
skylights. But her voice interrupted some

moment's divinity. It broke a spell
as surely as a teacher might clap chalk
dust out in clouds where coiled heads of Aeolic
papier-mâché columns wait in the dull

end of the day and the restless heads turn,
the black and gold braids of their thought fixed so
quickly elsewhere, turned to the vertigo
of pleasure, giving up the discipline

of what's created, as when each found shard
rose from the midden of the possible
and knit into curvaceous bloom, the vengeful
silence teased by approaching flutes a second

time—and a third. It lasts to our own day,
such rapture, gong-bright and gargantuan,
a heavenly joke, a dance, a festal throne;
then fades like all recovered symmetry.

# The Ballad of Gold

A man stood at the corner of Ninety-sixth Street,
shifting from leg to leg in the early cold
that would deepen with the blue December twilight,
and to the wind he said, "Buy gold, buy gold."

What he meant was, "We buy gold." His canvas apron
announced this plain and factual legend too,
in black and white, with block capitals like a headline:
CITY DEFAULTS ON ITS LOANS! KILLER ON FURLOUGH!

But the wind was the only thing at large that evening,
breathing over the bins of a superette nearby,
where the tubers twined with a bruised and hairy craving,
and the only gold was that of the evening sky,

where boiling clouds the color of day-old coffee
were split by glowing veins from Witwatersrand,
Colombia, Odendaalsrus, Armenia or Lydia,
all the distant points that had gathered and thickened

in the hawker's voice—though he need not have gone
    to the trouble,
for the rush hour crowds had descended long ago
to the subway and, in any case, beneath double
layers of ulster, alpaca or polyester,

the nine-to-fivers had nothing left to ransom
at the sunset gates, at the golden door of hope,
no richly worked heirloom, surpassingly handsome;
nothing but a strand of days in its broken loop

and the bankrupt feeling of another week beyond salvage.
However slight the margin he needed to survive,
the wind snatched it from his lips, took it on a voyage,
and changed every offer to an imperative

flung in his teeth. Though he sang like a
        white-throated sparrow
his intermittent ballad of works and days,
spring was months off, the gate of heaven narrow,
and, for all his mandrake promise, it was twenty degrees.

# Saint Rock



Man's best friend is—himself and the living God.
I, Saint Rock, stand accompanied by this
     shovel-jawed hound
with a loaf in his mouth. Admire the burl of my thighs,
the sinew of them, wrought from Norman poplars;

admire the extravagant brim of my rain-proof hat,
and the gold trees figured on crimson in my doublet,
and the soft leather of the purse I wear for alms.
I lived in the woods, content with the company of elms

and oaks wrought with ivy, apart from my own kind.
But still I caught the plague. Were it not for the bread
brought me by that strange dog, and his knowing tongue
strong in my groin, I would not have lasted long,

once the frightful buboes began to rise like knots
in pale wood, once my poor hermit's stock of nuts
and berries ran out, once I yielded to delirium.
But his affection healed me. It was sloppy and warm,

dogspittle the only balm in my century,
though our Savior spat on his hands at Bethsaida,
and the blind man said at first he saw walking trees.
Once I lived willingly far from the cities

of men, but later all my woods came alive
with citizens fleeing the plague. They were
    figments; to drive
them from my sight cost me this wound. See, I will show
it to you, my legging rolled down to just below

its red, red mouth. I am not a good man.
I love neither my woods nor being human.
I am Saint Rock. In the desolate wilderness,
my wound cries out that I was saved for this.

# The Daughter of Jairus

(MARK 5: 21–43)

Brushing the salt out of his hair, he strode
up from the port. People were everywhere,
murmuring, attentive, and expectant. Could
this really be the man the fearful Gada-

renes asked to leave their shores for what he did?
A slight man, dressed in robes of a mouse-brown,
amid the heat and stink of circumcised
crowds on a Mediterranean afternoon.

And then the ruler of the synagogue
approached, his robes splendid with blue and gold,
though dervishes of red dust seemed to clog
his voice. The other knew without being told

that Jairus' lovely daughter lay near death.
A shadow as of legions crossed his brow,
something black, porcine, a revulsion with
these people and their bodies and their low

despairs and fascinations; and the mob,
sensing this, pressed in closer, lest he should
abandon them. The virtue seemed to ebb
out of him for a moment, and he cried,

"Who touched me?" And they smiled behind their hands,
so drab the wool he wore, so rough the hem,
and his disciples said, "Master, with thousands
nearby, how can you ask who touches whom?"

36

Nonetheless his glance shot round, as if he
wondered, for just a moment—what's the use,
all the world being bought and sold routinely
in grief and covenants of faithlessness?

Then a woman stepped forward. Something in
her eyes, some unappeasable hunger
not wholly of the body, calmed his own
impatience and moved him with pity toward her.

She had touched him to find some end, some term
to her outrunning loneliness; she had
believed in him. With clamor all around them,
he dried the twelve-year fountain of her blood,

just as a servant came from Jairus' house,
breathless and bowing and a little pleased,
smug with the power that bad news confers,
and loudly whispered, "Alas, she is lost;

the girl is gone," waiting with solemn glee
to watch the crumbling of earthly pomp,
waiting for rank to relent tellingly
under this blow, ruler become a tramp,

ashes heaped on his smooth midrashic pate,
who had so doted on his only daughter.
But when the man in mouse-brown overheard it,
he looked with distaste at the messenger,

and to Jairus he said, "Only believe."
And so they came to a comfortable house
of modest frame and simple architrave,
the court filled with a funeral carouse

of instruments already. When the man
said, "Why this music? For she only sleeps,"
fiddles' arpeggios laughed him to scorn,
and the brass answered with loud farts and burps.

The girls' parents accompanied him inside,
into a room full of the smell of death.
He brushed away the small green fly that browsed
on her forearm, took her hand, and said, *"Talitha

cumi."* Nothing happened. The half-closed eyes
looked at him vulgarly, the girl's long hair
still wrought and parsed with sweat from her six days'
flux and the rackings of attendant fever.

Her body lay stone cold upon the narrow
bed, unreachable, beyond human thought:
too soon, he felt, for her spirit to follow,
however, and he settled down to wait.

And she, quite mesmerized with lamentations
from the yard outside (she was only twelve),
turned at last from the fluent musicians,
intrigued that this ordinary stranger should have

come to pay court just when she had decided
to slip away from her body and her
blood's thicknesses and the unmediated
storm of feelings that swept the calendar

of her no-more-than-ordinary life.
She sighed gently. The man in mouse-brown stood,
smoothed his coarse robes, swore Jairus and his wife
to silence about this, and then departed,

knowing full well how quickly they would talk,
unable to perceive the larger shape
behind such phenomenal rhetoric,
their hearts so doubtfully alive with hope;

and he destined for yet a little while
to give their sufferings a kind of order,
against brute intimations of the mortal
events that lay not far in his own future.

## Stanzas from the Life of George Fox, 1651–1662

*for Roberta Capers*

I came once to Lichfield.
    Rumour preceded me,
        the priests who said
        I had been taken up above the cloud,
    returned to earth gently,
my pockets filled with silver and with gold.

Three steeplehouses there
    struck at my very sight,
        past hedge and ditch,
        the whining of the shepherds' collie bitch,
    till quickly I untied
my shoes, the Lord's word in me like a fire,

and barefoot, crying "Woe!"
    and "Woe!" strode through the town
        of bloody Lichfield;
        and only learned a thousand had been martyred
    there under Diocletian
when my own blood had marked the crusted snow.

They could not then agree
    what to do. Some opined
        to have me up
        before their Parliament; others said ship
    him off to Ireland.
But praised or blamed is all the same to me.

And weary once I came
        to an house, it being night
                and wintery.
                But my plain speech took the woman strangely,
        and when I asked for meat,
she said she had none; when I asked for cream

(though I do not much like
        such food, only to test
                her honesty),
                she said no once again. So, to shape three
        denials in her breast,
I asked her then if I might have some milk,

and watched a young boy draw
        his fist reeking away
                from a stout churn
                when she had smoothly told me there was none.
        She blessed herself, and sorely
beat him, and banished me like an outlaw,

so that, three days from Christmas,
        a haystack snow and rain
                had long turned gray
                kept me and made my only bed till day,
        with voles and shrews and vermin,
with beaten straw and water's searching fingers;

in spite of which they claim
        my buttons are of silver
                (but alchemy
                is all they are) and exclaim, "Oh! See how he

shines! Oh! See how he glisters!"
when leather-suited George is all I am,

and was when Oliver
    Protector spoke with me.
        I tried to tell
        how Christendom has grown incapable
    of all true amity,
lacking the spirit which vouchsafed us Scriptures,

renewed in fellowship.
    He caught me by the sleeve
        the moment I
        turned from him, his eyes full, and said gently,
    "Could you and I but have
one hour a day together! For I hope

no more that ill befall
    you than it should my very
        soul." I replied
        (that lonely man hung on my every word)
    he would do well to pray
God soften his heart in the nation's counsel.

Yet he was full of pride,
    for when I saw him next
        and summoned him
        to put off the crown of this earthly kingdom,
    he became quickly vexed,
sat above me, and in a light voice said

that he would be as high
    in this world as I was,
        and laughed. But thus
        it proved: I saw him high on Tyburn gallows
    and rolled with infamies
into his grave by the new monarchy.

I lately had a vision
    of a great mastiff who
        would have bit me,
        but like Samson in the vineyard of Timnah,
    I rent him jaw from jaw.
So the Lord's power rends the Worldly One.

A bloody Emperor once
    at Nicomedia
        split mighty Rome.
        Between those jaws is hunger and
            Christ's Kingdom:
    captain, housewife, boy.
But the husbandman is to wait in patience.

# The Snow Sphinx

One evening—it will be just before winter's end,
your neighbor coughing all night in the room below,
who has aged forty years since December—
reading about Parian marble, your hearing will quicken
to the grain of ice lightly touching the window,
and so you will leave the quarries' translucent glitter,

the dream of a warmer climate, and go outside,
into the blizzard and the nighttime park,
where you will find on a bench a classical torso,
a minor miracle, adequately modeled,
a woman, high-breasted, the long line of her back
curving down, and her navel deep, and sculpted in snow.

You will think to yourself: she cannot last till morning,
naked as she is (though the crotches of trees are veiled,
and all the ledges of schist are blanketed under).
Frost crystals will stipple her flesh with scintillating
lights; she will seem like the matrix of the world,
daring the imagination to move beyond her—

but you will, past the priestess' cold thighs and ankles
and what they guard, for what crouches not far away
in the clotted dark is melancholy and superb:
a sphinx that has driven back the feathery rubble
of its own creation, tiny crocuses lighting the way
with their stalled blue jets of flame, as in a suburb

of hell, the cat's ears tufted, the mighty paws
crossed in repose, as if somehow to relax
the vigilance of its grief for the unnumbered dead;
a sphinx that turns the blind balls of its eyes
toward heaven, rough Babylonian locks
plaited in three around the horn on its forehead.

Where are the piles of skulls, the shattered femurs
with the marrow sucked out, the witless evidence
of questions tried but unanswered, all the human spasm
of doubt and panic? Where is the repeated curse
of ordinary wisdom defeated by sense,
the individual lives whose ending is the same?

A young man with a long mustache and a cleft chin—
in a moment you will recognize him: white,
immortal, still. In that moment he will speak,
his words caressing you like a ghostly tendon
of snow. Quick, quick! With the rising stink of wet
lawns closing on you, tell him: who made the snow sphinx?

# III

# $M$_emnon_

The pilot adjusts his Ray Bans
against the rapture of dawn's

low red sun, then takes a sip
of coffee and continues his equip-

ment check. This is the hour
when lovely Eos wept for

her child Memnon, comely and black,
slain by Achilles. The quick-

drying dew is her tears, or so
legend has it, shining on this Cairo-

or-elsewhere-bound widebody,
its engine pods precisely

centered over anthropomorphic
Kilroy shapes on the stained tarmac.

An elephant's trunk gropes and falls.
Held to the truth of its seals,

beauty stands in a desert place alone,
like, say, the Colossus of Memnon

which an earthquake or King Cambyses
once reduced to a seated, headless

figure, singing at the first touch
of daylight, a sound like the passage

of a hand across harpstrings, or
Memnon greeting his mother,

we are told (the empirical
say that air expands in the chill

pores of stone with the warmth of the sun)
—or the wail of a Pratt & Whitney engine.

Which souls are kept? Which are lost?
In this tableau, a French archeologist

talks with a soldier, a hookah
refreshes two men in the shadow,

and a camel waits ill-temperedly.
Inscriptions in Greek to the knee

praise, in sand-blasted hexameters,
an empire, *ses misères, ses splendeurs.*

But the pilot drawls on about azimuth
and poontang in the cockpit with

the copilot. He will keep his head,
even while the faithful press eastward

toward Mecca in unnumbered prayers
across the thwart sand (when they rise,

a few grains will cling on each brow,
blazing up like small jewels from the furrow

of their concentration and love).
He will conjure the mountain to move,

unfazed by distance or time,
secure in the formulas given him

less than a hundred years ago:
thrust, lift, drag, so combined with pure ego

that they cannot fail to outlast
love and monuments; or, at the worst,

if the dark ashes must whirl
high, as they did at the funeral

games of Memnon, then surely the fire
will round to birds' flight, bent together

over the sullen marshes,
and his soul in its apotheosis

will become a sky-tinged grain that lives
at the height for a moment, then moves

beyond vision or history
or the time zones of Europe and Africa.

# Rhône Valley, after Rain

Herons on Lac Léman wait
like English dowagers who've
just learned the Montreux Palace
has burned down again. In the
vineyards are laborers whose
slickers are bright against the
soil, like narcissus at Les
Pléiades. Hectare on hectare
of apricot and pear trees
glow incandescent at their
tips. These orchards were planted
by Rome, unmenaced by the
high scar of lasting snow or
the slurry of runoff past
the dogleg of the Rhône, where
gravity leaned on the plow
of a glacier and then changed
its mind, as if history
were no more than a gust of
wind across a dead lake, the
play of neural waves across
the chill gray flesh of a snail
on a window after rain,
the helplessness of tissue
caught in the harmony of
an idea realized,
not by the creature stalled in
its clear track of slime, but by
the thinker beyond the glass,
whose mind pursues the deep fretwork

of its channels, then pauses
and writes, *In fine vicissitude,
Beauty alternates with Grandeur,
as if Peace had established
herself in the Bosom of Strength.*

# The Transformation of Light

August in the Alps of Vaud:
the rain is sudden and drives vertical.
I watch the storm gather over the mountains I know:
Grand Muveran, Petit Muveran, Dents de Morcle;

and watch the cloud closing its empty fist,
as if the gneiss, in its plutonic weave,
were a napped cloth vastly caught in some outburst,
obliterating all for rage or love,

genealogy and profile lost, and then once more calm—
as it is sometimes with a family at supper,
though these are strangers who give me shelter from
the brief, irrational violence of weather.

He is something with the power authority,
distilling the cloudy water of the Rhône
into street lights that zigzag up from the valley.
Like a knot in the throat, I have passed the turbine

at a certain defile in the valley road
where the water drives hard into the flank of the hill,
is taxed in darkness and seethes from the louvered
gate to braid coldly onward over the gravel.

Noëmi has had her bath, his child of pleasure.
Her puptent sags out back. She is seven.
Her gold curls gleam like pyrite in the later
dusk given to those who live in the mountains.

In one hand she holds a *tartine*, in the other
a cup of milk disturbed by the sweet obsidian
of blackberries from the forest. Then it is her
bedtime. Her mother is living in Lausanne.

All night she will hear the wrinkled bulk of the glacier
debride the land with its knives of aquamarine,
with its pistol-shots of torsion. It is speaking to her,
she thinks, saying, Child, when will you be grown,

when will you be adept at the transformation
of light, as your father is, and lost to me?
In the morning, mist will rise through each black pine,
and childhood lift off her insensibly.

# Decline and Fall

(LAUSANNE, JUNE 1987)

The bower is long since demolished,
his friend's exquisite four acres,
the view shelving down by vineyard

and meadow to the sleeping lake.
The Federal Post Office Building
now covers the site, the acacias

gone, who knows, for khaki clothing
for the troops ground into dust,
the sepoys, an empire of words flung

to the banks of the Ganges, the conquest
of language complete two hundred years
ago in this orotund, vast

warning wrought in balanced phrases,
which has suffered no erosions,
just as the Alps remain stupendous,

rising through mist and the moon's silence
the mountains of Savoy,
from beyond which inspiration's

rebel drum came once, its tattoo of anarchy,
which stirred his blood and made him nervous,
who knew his importance in society

(he was banished here in disgrace)
was less a positive than a relative weight,
to be swept aside with eight days'

table linens or traded, the companionable light
of a fire for the invisible torpor
of a stove. He called his a "fortunate

shipwreck" on this lovely shore,
and earned his right to posterity
through long residence and decent behavior,

the miserable and the gorgeous authentically
mixed, the magazines of bacon, vinegar
and straw left in each frontier city,

the columns of Gordian's villa, which were
done in four kinds of marble,
or the cruelty with which an empire

learns it is incapable
of further change, as Plautianus,
for example, in order to fill

the train of eunuchs at his daughter's
wedding, castrated one hundred
free-born Romans, husbands and fathers.

The lake gilds the coast eastward
toward dawn, and history
delivers a bachelor in the splendid

Eden of his mind, a solitary
who has worked the original soil
thirty years, conscious of mortality

in the barbarous world of which exile
and his English birth have made him the center,
like success at love almost accidental,

or the play of the body, which has meant failure
at fencing and dancing and horseback,
and brings death in his fifty-sixth year.

# Saint Nicholas

(ZÜRICH, 6 DECEMBER)

Whether a man hired from town or the father of friends,
he would come every year and speak in a booming voice,
his shirt unbuttoned, his fingers nicotine-stained,
quite recognizable beneath his disguise,

in the way that something you have done but are not proud
of stays at the back of your mind even when you are
doing something else, and weighs like a sack of gold,
or the bag of fugitive apples he spilled on the floor;

tangerines with a pungent chill on them, to roll
under the furniture; chambered nuts, their meat
wrapped in a bitter membrane and their shells
pitted like old blades; or the sticky dates

that took the carpet's wool as a wound does lint.
How eagerly we browsed on this edible clutter
on our hands and knees! Not without wounds, without
    limit,
without memory, even as children how well we under-

stood that when we looked up, he would be gone,
having left behind a golden homunculus
(modeled of yeast and flour) in the kitchen
with a flail of twigs in one hand, to take its place

behind the steam pipe for another year,
coming down like the anger in our mother's voice,
thickening each feast of ours into remorseful clabber,
haling us out of our childhood avenues

of smoky nut-meats, sweet dates and lights of citrus,
teaching us greater joy beneath the flail,
surrendering our flesh so that conscience might release us,
and our thoughts, like Saint Nicholas, become visible.

# *The Crocus*

It's all the talk of Zürich
(at lunch in *Zum Safran,*
where the Gewürztraminer
is drunk mostly by men):

how, last night, kids with crimson
paint spattered the old choir
of Zwingli's church, so that it
streams like an abattoir.

Inside, an earnest preacher
inquires, with Saint John,
"Who is to blame for blindness,
the parents or the children?"

He does not know the answer,
but quotes Ezekiel:
"A father drinks his vineyard's
fruit with contentment, while

the tannin in the same cup
makes his son cough and frown,
for whom no trick of racking
will clear the ruined wine."

But wherein lies their failure,
the elders? Did they not
guard their frontiers from Germans,
Italians and whatnot

through two world wars and after,
from every darker shade
of skin and attitude, from
all that was not Swiss-made?

Has peace not breathed, a fragile
exhausted deity,
inside these rocky borders
throughout one century

and back six more? Or almost—
though Zwingli wears the furred
gown of a scholar, Bible
in one hand, there's a sword

clenched in the other. He died
resisting popery,
a man of principle, a
Reformer, Ulrich Zwingli,

who would have known his mind when
youth seemed to fight it out
with age, as in our own day;
who would have known, no doubt,

though Giacometti's windows
might subtly romanize
the pure plain beams of daylight,
that he must yet despise

them for their different beauty,
so ready to seduce
the mortal heart with hopeless
fantasies of peace,

just as the nightly penman,
in weeping capitals,
has scrawled WHAT IF NOBODY
COMES, NEXT TIME A WAR CALLS?

The city is in turmoil:
keffiyehs, paving stones,
teargas, round wicker shields and
windowless gray vans,

till, in one burst shopwindow,
the idle breeze plays with
a phrase torn from its binding:
"Custom should yield to truth."

The elders pause, then hazard
a countertactic rich
with promise for the future
(just the same future which

they stand accused of selling
by their daughters and sons).
Their new campaign is—planting
crocuses on the lawns.

BLOSSOM, DON'T BURN! their posters
announce. THE CROCUS! Such
a mania for planting,
like tulips to the Dutch.

What are they, Greens? Anarchists
and nodding addicts smile
at this surpassing quaintness:
*Gopferdehlino'hmal!*

Even in this small kingdom,
no one can wait till spring
for methadone, satori,
freedom, or anything

like reconciliation,
when each small purple flame
creeps unseen through the city,
ambiguously calm.

## Dents du Midi

Each day brings back the chiseled peaks of stone
across the valley. They will never change
their shape, not to the hundredth generation
after mine, but offer the eye the same crude edge,

morning and evening: thorn to tear the blush
of momentary feeling; a dark head
bent over its own lap, hearing the rush
of loneliness through pinions as a buzzard

spirals down through ten thousand feet of air,
but still unmoved, cruel, fixed in its own thought;
chisel to break a dome of many colors;
hook to draw the world out, or horn to end it;

perpetual, bent on asymmetry
and primal strength frozen in a lean crouch.
The last hut's tin roof twinkles in the high
cold like the fire opal in a brooch

set artfully upon a skirt of broad
glaciers. The white stream's "thread of broken purpose"
leaks from a ribbed cavern long set to guard
uncounted generations of lost climbers,

releasing one man from the early Bronze Age
miraculously, four thousand years later,
his arrows all unfledged, no signs of damage,
having traversed the ice-fields of eter-

nity to find the still-unchanged tableau
I look at, thinking my gift of perspective
defines it—but it does not. What he saw,
when he looked as I do and was alive,

nowhere included him. My life's too quick;
my grief's too warm. My children's children's eyes
will never wash this tribal order back
to where it first rose from the covering seas.

# *For the Assassins*

(AIR-INDIA FLIGHT 182, JUNE 23, 1985)

A young helicopter
pilot feathers his star
of rotors, jumps down and, across the whining air,

shouts that there is a mile-
long slick due south of Kinsale,
on which he saw, as if it rode upon a shell,

the figure of an archer
painted on a hatch cover.
He says there is no sign of any survivor,

although the bodies will
rise, battered by their fall
five miles and more and, like a venial

inspector, the Atlantic
will now and then give back
shoes, wallets, seat cushions, perhaps a pocketbook:

summary evidence,
investigated since
by those fantastic worms whose lightless phosphorescence

trails through the numbered rows,
indifferent to those
still waiting in their belted postures of repose.

The turbine blades outside
bend like a many-petaled
flesh-eating flower; having found the water, sucked

*67*

and filled, they rest now. The
wing flaps are cunningly
extended still, to let the aircraft down more gently,

and the smooth metal skin,
once dappled by the sun
and cloud, is slowly anodized by the saline

and superhuman weight
that burst the delicate
expensive dials glowing and wavering in the cockpit,

and made the needles plunge
into an extreme range
infinite beyond numbers and beyond language

with which to claim intent
in this, or some triumphant
purpose, beyond the welter of mere accident,

or vindicate one cause
above all the others.
Although instead it is simply notorious,

what they have done will not
go by, for it has brought
the heart, from being appalled, closer to dull habit.

# IV

# Articulate Nature

Spit-globes in the unmown field stain your pants'
leg, as you walk by, with morphemes of drool.
Butterflies climb the air in breathless feints,
their wings brocaded in saffron and coal,

matched like the power grids of a nighttime city,
having left the Siberian iris where they rested,
studying the vellum petals' still-undry
watercolors, delicately veined and freckled.

There is some lesson here, some fluent clause,
unknown to you and yet colloquial
elsewhere: the field mouse that soaked the "Peerless"
trap in the basement last night with its small

blood knew it; phoebe chicks overlapped in
their nest built in the ripening currant bush
(woven of twigs and fiberglass insulation),
blind as they are, already know it much

better than you do; and the golden fox
that will pause like the idol of a kingdom,
superb and extinct, as he trots across
the evening road, guarding a stillness in him

that makes your own seem like a rude commotion,
will know it too. Only you will not hear
that divine sentence, though you watch and listen,
late student come to articulate nature.

# Between *Roscoe* and *Absarokee*

We are deceived by history. America had a great spirit given to freedom but
it was a mean, narrow, provincial place; it was NOT the great liberty-loving
country, not at all. Its choice spirits died.     —W. C. WILLIAMS


This was the hour to shun fighting, when a
moccasin sole, soft with dew, absorbed the
thorn of the prickly pear, when the bowstring,
made of animal tendon, went slack too.

Somehow imagination still wakes, or
sleeps only lightly under a veil of
Prozac, cigarettes, cheap wine, and the pink
flowers of sainfoin. Those blurred white shapes in

the twilight where the aboriginal
herds once numbered sixty million could be
purebred Maremma hounds guarding their flocks
of sheep, or something else. (A year later,

George Herendeen "thought the General's corpse
had been torn apart by wolves.") In places,
the dead face of the land seems to yawn at
the rich parquet of strip farming, butcher-

block panels alternating the colors
of buffalo wool caught on a strand of
barbed wire with the straw color of an
arrogant hero's scalp, and not even

the druid circles of central pivot
irrigation can recover what is
gone. Now and then a plow furrow turns up
a stone flesh scraper with the odor of

carrion still heavy upon it, of
irreconcilable differences,
and where piled stones made a fire circle, place
of first menstruation or vision lodge

two thousand years ago, a woman will
bend in the morning to gather scarlet
false mallow and mariposa lily.
This is the hour when the arrow hawk drops

toward fireflies braiding a garment of
light in the river bottom; when Reno's
troopers piled bags of bacon, hay and oats
as best they could into a primitive

breastwork, a counterfeit of abundance,
and considered the sounds of night, the wolf's
howl, the hoot of an owl (or the sound of
a hundred freight cars passing eastward on

the uncontested rails drifted over
on sidings with hard red winter wheat), sounds
too perfect to be other than human
imitations of what was once a great

wilderness. They lay awake, thinking and
trying to remember the place any
of them had come from, but without success,
and waited with dread for the rising dawn.

# *Martinique*

*for Aimé Césaire*

The chough and sibilance of tide
    surges and falls.
A rainbow's braced across the arid west,
    spectral and sure,
    banding infinities—

*métisse, griffe, mulatresse, chabine,*
    *quarteronne, capresse—*
names which have passed from custom, though the blood
    remembers them
    like steps of an old dance.

The mangrove seed that drops upright
    into the mud
with time grows into low elaborate
    root lattices,
    in which the *cestmafaute*

hides with its white fist clenched against
    all predators
(the pinch of conscience, genealogy),
    like a thorned heart,
    the fig of Barbary's

bruised purple fruit, being hollowed out
    by a small bird
that sings, *Do you eat from fine china or*
    *plain earthenware*
    *or maybe calabash?*

The green roots search for difference
        but can find none;
the Creole women, dressed *à l'impératrice*
        with madras turbans,
        their earlobes pendent with

fasces and cylinders of gold,
        more splendid than
high-breasted alabaster Josephine,
        are dust now; the
        *maisons de rendez-vous*

and all their pleasures calcined by
        refining fire
from the shape-changing mountain in the year
        1902,
        as if that world had been

transmuted to a raddled drool
        of sun across
the widest leaves, distilled in amber tears
        of gum that shine
        (the forest is all eyes)

on a sweet split trunk, populous
        with honeybees
and loud above the jawbone of a goat.
        Yet mingled in
        the streets of old St. Pierre

were darkling smells of sugar and
    raw garlic, while
the sounds of travail played beneath the sweet
    continuous
    music of rushing streams

that fed the black bronze tritons and
    the dusky swans
in many fountains. Now, where gray doves browse,
    a theater's
    ruined mosaic floor

beneath prismatic tints and wide
    lava banquettes
shows gray doves browsing, whose parodic calm
    endures the claim
    of years murmurously.

The lance-head viper waits just past
    the tended lawn,
hidden by flowers of the wild plantain,
    each jagged chevron
    bloody with sacrifice.

Then a sweet fume of cooking fires.
    This paradise
is a man-trap, urging forgetfulness
    and sensual ease
    stealthily, by degrees,

until the green joints of bamboo
    explode nearby
like small-arms fire in a restive city,
    waking to this,
    waking to history,

to twilight, when the frog tunes his
    small voice to the
deep well of the past: de Gaulle and Lumumba,
    black or *béké*,
    Carib or Arawak,

unreconciled. The rays of the
    declining sun
light modest pastel houses on the hillside
    beautifully
    just at the end of day.

# Two Tidal Sonnets

## 1. Ludovisi Throne

The Queen of Love was born out of the tide
(so legend tells), and learned those rhythms first,
cut static from the foam of mackerel-sided
swells, all creation in her like a thirst.
Apparently she was fond of the smell
of brine, fond of small swarming birds and flowers.
She had no memory of pain at all,
but felt the distance of remembered pleasures.
Valved like a conch, her smile archaic, she
moved with a single salt imperative
toward the shore, her perfect nudity
a weight to make the rainbowed shell's lip dive
and tremble gladly underneath her feet,
desire still just a vague unease—the slight
asymmetry of new sharp breasts a girl
gracefully stoops to dress in pleats of wool.


## 2. Moonrise, Indian Wells Beach, Amagansett

The hoops of salt thresh up the sloping beach,
bubbling and staining, and our feet weave through
the brown sand. She moves just out of my reach,
a slip of blue beside the greater blue.
We stop a moment, and I say, "I love you."
From the loud mulch of surf, a tumbled plank
backstrokes heavily, and a sodden clew
of weed hangs briefly on the graveled flank
of tide that roars and sucks our footsteps blank,

retreating with a phosphorescent hiss.
It is not true. Or it is. From a bank
of cloud, the moon rises and calmly rises,
urging on the rhythmic advance of brine
and heave of darkness, a high androgyne.

# *Lest He Put Forth His Hand*

Down at the ocean's chop shop, I was,
  wondering where the prime mover might
    have got to, who had been absent some
  time, to judge by that old engine block
coughing brackish water, listing on

its bed of rockweed, with every gear
  and lever seized with rust. There were crab
    claws, bleached to just the shades of kitchen
  enamel, and a chesty, pecked-out
carapace; rounded periwinkle

and tiny bladders of weed with hooks;
  beaded minarets of sea urchin
    and the smashed helices of a drill;
  there were mussel shells, sprung open, blue
like a bad stomach, and razor clams;

there was bottle glass, fogged with constant
  motion, and a bit of stoneware with
    a curd of cloud across it, like a
  moment's weather, a lustrous edge of
quahog-purple, rolled back across the

sky, causing the shore to gleam where it
  was sown with earholes and arabesques,
    all listening for the return of
  life back through the lattices of bone-
salt toward component time; but what

I heard was not the desultory
        pop and sputter of the primeval
            mud sucking its gums under the ebb
        tide, but rather a ruined voice that
coasted down in the scented quiet

from the nearest mossy fir-top or
        stumbled over the glittering scales
            of the water. It must have been at
        just the hour that God is said to have
walked in the cool of the day and called

in His garden that the blue heron
        lit and flared his gorget of feathers
            (neck like a sink joint or the stomach's
        duodenal curve) and began to
compose one image from so many

broken hungers, to strike and strike at
        what lay behind, being fed by this,
            burning, diesel-blue, across the tide
        like some angel's sword, turning against
those who might once have lived forever.

# The Spider's Art

The spider's art lies in a knowing distance
from what it most desires. Here is a wasp
caught, all unwittingly, upon the cusp,
the midair point, of fatal circumstance.

Colored like earwax and old fingernails,
long abdomen and a deep greyhound chest,
isinglass wings invisibly distressed,
its athlete's body hesitates, then struggles.

Too late! The spider comes on gay striped legs,
throwing its countless hoops of sticky thread
around a nightmare shape it will avoid
touching, for all that the wasp heaves and drags

and glistens in its labor to be free.
The spider, physicist and acrobat,
has measured out eight times precisely what
will be required, and knows the intimacy

of last embraces can wait until later.
For now, it's knit one, purl one, on and on,
rhythm translated as slow suffocation.
To sleep, then feed: that is the way to prosper.

And when another spider twice its size
blunders too near, with dauntless tally-ho
it straitjackets this cousin-german too.
The bonds of kin yield to biology's

conniving hunger and disloyal web.
These dried-out husks, belayed to a dark corner,
become parts of a rough material anchor
for the known world. From the egg sac's gray orb

suspended there, each tiny spideret
begins life with an inborn confidence
in its own legs, against the evidence
of something much larger and hostile to it,

until, the summer people gone, a girl
arrives, and with one stroke of her worn broom
moves on, indifferent, to another room,
the torn gauze breathing like a parable.

# *Aubade, Deer Isle*

The pilot light shines up through each stove ring
with crowns of flame, hours before breakfast
on our last day. The refrigerator is purring;
the calendar is still turned to August,

six years ago (a Currier and Ives
rotogravure—"A Harbor For The Night"—
in which three boatmen think about their lives
around a campfire in the river's quiet,

their vessel pulled up safely on the shore,
their dinner warming as a cloud of smoke
billows to keep insects from where they are.
A piece of bread, some succotash, and talk . . .)

What is potential in life? What is static?
Dawn rises like a godhead newly come
across the endless drift of the North Atlantic,
past Gander and St. John, past the bald dome

of Cadillac and Mount Katahdin's knife-edge,
at last flooding the modest eastern wall
of our neighbor the lobsterman's cottage,
already painted a glad deferential

pink, as if the warmth of that rendezvous
lingered with memory and anticipation.
Light wakes, a child, before its parents do,
unreconciled to their complete exhaustion.

We sleep on into morning and ignore
the squirrel that shouts from the cleft of a tree—
a marriage still bedridden at this hour!
A mourning dove chants in the hoops of blackberry;

a blue heron patiently stalks the runoff
and cold mud, back this year from Florida,
his body a poised interrogative,
bleached shades lighter, it seems, by what he saw

down South. Meanwhile, out in the sagging barn,
freed from all human shackles and restraints
by the nocturnally clever raccoon,
garbage will be festooned in the strong tints

of its corruption, a black lace of plastic,
a gash of lobster shells, a smell of fish,
something to contemplate moon-eyed, ecstatic,
intent. And then we will get up and wash.

Maps on the wall give soundings at mean low
water: shoals, islets, countless as the dried
blood-colored explosions of mosquito
left by some tenant on the fiberboard.

On the untended lawn, a little iron
grill limps on broken legs, its belly full
of ashes, like the gray and distant town
that draws us back with mild calendrical

imperatives, grateful for nothing worse:
weddings, routine appointments, a birthday.
It's breakfast time. For a moment we pause
and taste a hunger like expectancy

of something to be done before the year
is out, something that sleeves the running tide
in muscular crystal and, miles from here,
still sees that cottage turn its pastel side.

*September, 1991*

# Interior, Sunday Afternoon

The pigeons make their sounds
"of burbling water and wood twisting in wood";
but the water never reaches the far disc of light,
and the traveler never climbs off the axle tree.

Not that there are not a hundred reasons to move;
but the brick is still learning blindness, sixty years on,
in that healed window-arch, and the cataracts stood like
     shields
in the eyes of a woman led through the greenmarket

at just the pace that pure sunlight yaws into shade
across the bedspread and scatters flakes of deep color
in prisms on the wall and lights a silk map there,
but without true destination. For you are home.

p. 5   "Hudson, P.Q., Canada." Isambard Kingdom Brunel (1806–1859) was an English civil engineer whose works included an ocean-going steamship, *The Great Eastern*, the largest steam vessel of its time.

p. 21   "Natural History." As in the unreliable but fascinating *magnum opus* of Pliny the Elder (c. 23–79 A.D.).

p. 56   "Decline and Fall." "His friend's exquisite four acres . . ." Georges Deyverdun, who with Suzanne Curchod was one of the people closest to Edward Gibbon.

p. 65   "Dents du Midi." Mountains in the Canton of Vaud in French Switzerland.

p. 72   "Between Roscoe and Absarokee." This poem is set in south-central Montana and refers in part to the events at the Little Bighorn River on June 25, 1876.

p. 75   "Martinique." The *cestmafaute* is a crab so called because of its habit of holding one outsize claw close to its body, as if beating its breast.